# Guide Library

Hillwood Museum
Washington, D.C.

COLLECTORS' PIECES 8

# ENGLISH CRYSTAL GLASS

John Bedford

WALKER AND COMPANY
NEW YORK

Library of Congress Catalog Card Number: 67-11600

First published in the United States of America in 1967 by Walker and Company, a division of Publications Development Corporation



*Printed in Great Britain*

# Contents

# Introduction

There is nothing in the world quite like glass, and nothing in the world of glass which is quite like English crystal glass of lead. Other countries may show glass with more spectacular and fantastic forms, more sophisticated decoration, more unerring perfection in making; but their material has nothing like the brilliance and internal fire of the English metal. Nor have their glassmen shown so much genius in taking ideas from Italy, Germany, the Netherlands or wherever, and yet producing a coherent and very real native style. It is a faculty which they have shared with the English potters and, in fact, is to be seen all through English artist-craftsmanship.

This little book tries to give a summary of the ways in which all this came about, and to show the kind of things which our glassmen made as the result. The term English Crystal has been preferred to 'flint glass' for three persuasive reasons. First, that when George Ravenscroft led a revolution in English glassmaking—about the same time as the English were having a revolution in their politics—he was seeking 'a particular sort of Crystalline glass resembling Rock Crystal': in other words he sought an English improvement on Venetian *cristallo*. Second, his famous glass of lead soon abandoned the use of flint and therefore made the term obsolete; and third, the word crystal is still used by the English glassblowers to describe the glass they make today and sell all over the world, using much the same methods and means as did their ancestors. In fact, one could offer the embryo collector no better advice than that he should start his researches in the glasshouses where English crystal began.

# 1. The Metal

Glass, which we take so much for granted in our everyday life, is a material with many remarkable and unique qualities. It can be found as a black stone called obsidian—there is a mountain full of it in the Yellowstone National Park. It also appears naturally as rock crystal, a form of quartz, which for centuries has been carved by craftsmen into precious and beautiful objects.

But man has found that in these forms he cannot realize the full potentialities of glass; so, taking ordinary materials like sand, soda, lime, lead and the ashes of plants and trees, he has produced a far more versatile and resourceful substitute. It can be blown, moulded into a thousand delightful shapes and decorated with carving, engraving, etching and painting; it can catch, retain and reflect light and colour as no other substance. There is even a sense in which it can be regarded not as a solid at all, but as a suspended or cooled liquid like ice. Connoisseurs know that if you rub a scratched piece sympathetically and skilfully it will go a little way back along the road to its molten state and swallow up its own scratches.

### SYRIA AND EGYPT

The story is told by Pliny—and it has been repeated many times since—that in classical times, a party of Phoenician sailor merchants went ashore and camped on a sandy beach by the mouth of the River Belus in Syria. In setting up their campfire they used some small rocks of a form of carbonate of soda from the cargo they were carrying, and when the fire cooled in the morning, they found that the soda had fused the sand beneath it into a kind of glass. This may well be a story invented to explain a known fact, but it was probably in some such way that the discovery of

a. *Anglo-Venetian goblet of the type made in London in the late sixteenth century by Giacomo Verzelini and engraved with diamond points. 5⅛ in.* b. *English or Netherlandish goblet, late seventeenth century.* 8 *in.* c. *Wine glass with inverted baluster stem and folded foot.* c. *1685. 5⅛ in.* d. *Wine glass with long bucket bowl gadrooned at base and wrythen baluster stem.* c. *1685. 5½ in.*

fusible glass was made. It is also a fact that that particular region was closely identified with some of the earliest known glass in the form we now know it. The Syrians and the Egyptians were the first of the great glassmakers, and their work is still to be seen in our museums. The Romans, learning from the Syrians and then from the Alexandrians, were also magnificent glassmakers, perhaps as good as any of those who followed them, but when they left the shores of England, never to return, there remained behind only a tradition. In the Dark Ages which followed, any glass made here would have been scarcely distinguishable from the *Waldglas* of Germany and the *verre de fougère* of France. This 'forest glass' was a greenish or brownish metal in which silica from sand was fused by potash from the ashes of beechwood or bracken. It seems to have been made here from the twelfth century onwards by craftsmen from Normandy, Lorraine and Flanders, who settled wherever they could find good and plentiful supplies of their materials and fuel—for example, the Weald of Kent and Sussex, the Forest of Dean and the country around Stourbridge. In the succeeding centuries many of these families left their slowly anglicizing names—Hennezel (Henzey or Ensell), Thisac (Tyzack), Thietry (Tittery) and Houx (Hoe)—in the parish registers of these districts.

## VENETIAN 'CRISTALLO'

In the meantime, the Romans had also bequeathed their art to the Venetians, who raised it to a peak of splendour such as had never been seen in the world before. Like other countries, England, with the new prosperity of a rising mercantile and maritime power, was in the market for something more luxurious than the native product, and it fell under the spell of the nearly colourless *cristallo*, or crystal glass, of Venice.

Named after the rock crystal which had always been the ideal of the early glassmakers, this *cristallo* found its silica not in sand, but in ground pebbles won from river beds. Its soda came from the ashes of marine plants (rather like our glasswort) called barilla, and its lime was derived from ground sea-shells and marble. By varying the proportions of these materials the men of the Venetian island of Murano could do practically what they liked with their metal; they could fashion it with the blowing iron and other traditional tools into a hundred lovely and fantastic forms apparently designed solely for the purpose of defying the fragility and delicacy of the substance.

The Venetians exported their *cristallo* to every country which could afford to buy it; they also—though much against their inclinations and their laws—exported some of their workmen, who carried the tradition of glass-making *à la façon de Venise* throughout Europe. Other countries followed the Venetian tradition so closely, in fact, that today it is sometimes very difficult to know just where, outside Venice itself, a particular object was made. For example, some of those pieces now labelled as Netherlandish *façon de Venise*—meaning that they were made in the Low Countries in the Venetian fashion—may very well have been made in England.

Italian glassblowers were working permanently in England by 1570, when Giacomo Verzelini (1523–1606) settled in London and obtained from Elizabeth I a licence to stay in England for twenty-one years and teach Englishmen how to make Venetian *cristallo*. He was followed by a succession of monopolists like Sir Robert Mansell, a retired admiral, who not only controlled glasshouses under licence from the Crown but also had the sole right of importing glass from Venice itself.

That a great deal was made here, however, we know from still extant records. John Greene, a London glass retailer who bought his supplies from the Venetian glassmaker Morelli, sent along with his orders the most exacting instructions and sketches of the kinds of glasses he required. From these we get a very good idea of the forms favoured in England in the late seventeenth century, as shown on page 6.

## ENGLISH CRYSTAL

The monopolists faded from the picture soon after the Restoration, and their place as entrepreneurs between the London glasshouses and the public was taken over by the London Glass Sellers' Company, who also exerted a great deal of influence on the provincial makers. Given a new charter by Charles II in 1664 they quickly went about the task of building up a native industry which would leave them less dependent upon expensive wares imported from Venice. Perhaps it was they who inspired the translation into English in 1662 of the standard work on glassmaking, Antonio Neri's *L'Arte Vetraria*.

It was certainly the London Glass Sellers' Company who some years later found and adopted as their chief artificer in the production of English glass a former shipowner in the Italian trade named George Ravenscroft, who had recently set up a glasshouse in London. This was about the year 1673, when Ravenscroft took out a patent for his 'particular sort of Crystalline glass resembling rock crystal'. A year or two later, he had engaged to sell the whole of his output to the company, and also to build for them another glasshouse, to be used for experimental work, in the quiet and seclusion of Henley-on-Thames, thirty-five miles west of London and thus hidden away from curious eyes.

Employing Italian-trained glassmakers from the Netherlands and elsewhere, Ravenscroft began his search for a metal which could be made independently of foreign materials and yet have the same qualities as the Venetian product, especially its immense facility of working.

At first he ran into difficulties, perhaps arising from the use of English burnt and ground flints in place of the Italian *cògoli* or pebbles. He then increased his proportion of potash and soda, so improving the metal's ductility, but this led to the serious defect known as 'crizzling', whereby a glass crazes into tiny cracks and can eventually disintegrate altogether.

GLASS OF LEAD

Undiscouraged, however, Ravenscroft introduced into his mixture a quantity of oxide of lead, following the ancient practice in Syria and Alexandria in making the glass 'paste' used for artificial gems. By the year 1676 he was able to announce that 'the defect of the flint glasses (which were formerly observed to crissel and decay) had been overcome'. Twelve months later he boldly advertised the slogan: 'No crissling or money returned'. As a result the glassmakers proudly and gratefully authorized

*Covered jug in Ravenscroft's glass of lead, with gadroons 'nipt diamond waies' and encircled with trailed decoration.* c. *1685. 11½ in.*

Ravenscroft to place a seal on his work impressed with the head of a raven, still to be seen on many extant pieces, notably that on page 9.

In fact Ravenscroft had not entirely solved the problem of crizzling, for most of the surviving examples of his work show traces of it, some quite heavy. But his successors, by increasing the amount of lead still further, did manage to eradicate it altogether.

Thus was born the new perfected glass of lead. It was much heavier in weight than the Venetian *cristallo*, and so could not be blown as thinly. But it was slower in action than its rival—it did not cool so quickly—and thus could be worked over a longer time. This was a quality which, as we shall see, suited the temperament of the English and Italo–English glassmakers better than the earlier short-lived soda glass. The lead glass also had a great brilliance, a liquidity which gave it a richness far exceeding the Venetian metal, and a peculiar and unique quality for holding and dispersing light, which, when it was faceted and cut, gave it even superior decorative qualities to rock crystal itself.

As noted in the Introduction, it has been called flint glass from Ravenscroft's original source of the silica; but within only fifty years, when glassmakers started to use sand, this term was to become obsolete. The words 'glass of lead' have been used by commentators to distinguish it from the potash glass of the Continent.

*Goblet with trailed 'nipt diamond waies' decoration carrying a fourpenny piece of 1697 in its stem.* (British Museum.)

# 2. The Early Styles

## ENGLISH BAROQUE

English crystal was born into an age of elaborate decoration. The silver of the day was ornately chased and embossed, furniture was opulently proportioned and richly carved, furnishings were stiff with embroidery and jewels. It would have been surprising if the work of Ravenscroft and the host of English glasshouses which sprang into existence in his wake had not reflected this taste very strongly.

But although the forms they used were still substantially Venetian in inspiration, the means they used to decorate their pieces was quite different. To demonstrate this, it may be helpful to give some idea of what went on—and still very largely does—in glassmaking.

In a typical glasshouse—and there are several in Stourbridge and Brierley Hill where the visitor is welcomed today—you will find that the 'pots' full of molten glass are arranged around a central furnace. The gaffer or his 'servitor' (note the survival of the French term) goes to the gloryhole and takes from it on the end of his blow-iron a 'gather' of hot glass, which he shapes by blowing it out into a bubble, swinging it about, rolling it up and down on his marver or smooth iron table, or perhaps blowing it directly into a mould, so that it takes up a required shape or surface pattern.

According to what is being made, proceedings now vary, but the piece may be transferred on to an iron rod called a pontil or puntee, which the gaffer can use for taking things a stage further. He can sit in his 'chair' rolling the rod up and down on its iron-clad arms, always keeping it on the move, and as he does so cutting it into shape with shears, manipulating it with various tools, and where required adding pieces of fresh glass which have been brought to him

*Posset pot and cover, ornamented with gadrooning and prunts.* (Saffron Walden Museum.)

by his 'servitor'. The process, it will be seen, calls for understanding teamwork, an innate sense of rhythm and an eye for form. In the glassmaking districts they say that either you have these qualities or you haven't.

With the rapidly cooling Venetian *cristallo* the blow-iron was all-important: given this material and this tool you could achieve the complex and delicate forms for which Venice was famous. But, as already noted, the English lead crystal, being slower to cool, did not seem to be suited to such immediate manipulation. Instead, the gaffers preferred to sit in their chairs and express their idea of beauty by trailing glass threads around a piece in lines or festoons, or by nipping these with tweezers into diamond or other shapes. They made up stems in openwork, stuck on elaborate finials, made their rims lobed, added basket work, pulled out wings with pinchers or stuck on small round lozenges called 'prunts'. Examples are shown opposite and on pages 9 and 10.

In a way, this form of decoration—hyaloplastic as it has been called—was very much the same sort of thing that was being done with pottery in London and Staffordshire at that time. In fact there are posset pots in earthenware with precisely similar forms to those in glass. It suited mightily a race of men, who, though often of foreign extraction, had been in England for several generations and had picked up the slower-moving ways of this country. Over a period of thirty or forty years it gave us some remarkable pieces; they were unlike anything made elsewhere and remained a total expression of their age.

But times were changing, and with them tastes: instead of the elaborate carving in oak, the sleek surface of walnut; in place of the rich ornament of Stuart silver, the simple elegance of the Queen Anne teapot. Staffordshire slipware had given way to the elegance of delftware and the refinement of saltglazed stoneware.

Alongside the baroque grandees, less elaborate forms were being developed for everyday use—drinking and sweetmeat glasses, jugs, bowls, and the like. They were simpler in style than the Venetian types specified by John Greene, and they foreshadowed the next development in glass.

Its outstanding feature was the baluster stem. The glassmakers had borrowed this form from Renaissance architecture, and by playing an infinity of variations on it, and combining it with different kinds of bowls and feet, they produced a remarkable range of glasses. These will be described in their place (page 38).

At first the forms followed the precept of Lord Shaftesbury, one of the chief spokesmen for the new taste: 'It is not the Bulk of a Fabrick, the Richness and Quantity of the Materials, the Multiplicity of the Lines, nor the gaudiness of the finishing that gives the Grace of Beauty and Grandeur to a building; but the Proportion of the parts to one another and to the Whole, whether entirely plain or enriched with a few ornaments properly disposed.'

The transition to the simpler and more classical forms was made easier by the brilliant texture of the new glass of lead, with its wonderful properties for retaining and dispersing light. These early balusters give us, no less effectively than the silver and furniture of the day, the restraint and disciplined good taste of what is called the Queen Anne style, though not very accurately for it began well before that lady's reign. As well as being the classical era of English crystal glass it was perhaps the apogee of English applied art.

*The baluster stem, with trumpet bowl and folded foot. Early eighteenth century. 7 in.* (Victoria & Albert Museum.)

## GERMAN INFLUENCES

But no sooner was Queen Anne dead than decoration began to flourish. The first move in this direction seems to have occurred with the arrival in London in 1709 from Germany of a large consignment of glasses of a type not seen here before. There were beer and wine glasses, tumblers, jellies and the like, all cut and carved in a manner entirely new to the natives.

They represented the upsurge in Europe of a new and vigorous glass-making industry which wanted to strike out in a different line from the Venetians by making greater use of cut and carved decoration; and they made a profound impression in the English capital. The London Glass Sellers were so alarmed, in fact, that they organized a ruckus at the public sale and managed to get it closed down. But this only made matters worse, for the glass was sold off to the public at a very cheap price and became exceedingly popular.

As the most conspicuous feature of the previous age was the baluster, so the new one produced the shouldered Silesian stem—a misleading term, for glasses of this kind were made not only in Silesia, but elsewhere in Central Europe. It is shown on this page and consists of a column of glass with a projecting shoulder at the top tapering away to the base and shaped in various ways.

*The Silesian stem, with round funnel bowl and folded foot.* c. *1710.*
(Victoria & Albert Museum.)

The Silesian stem appeared not only on drinking glasses, but also on sweetmeat glasses, candlesticks, salvers, fruit dishes and the like, where it lingered much longer—in fact throughout the eighteenth century. Its indubitably Teutonic feeling struck quite a new note among styles which had so far largely been inherited from the Latin taste, and its establishment in England was perhaps helped by the German race of kings who had ascended the British throne. But, once in the hands of the English gaffers, it underwent the usual sea-change; and wonderful were the ways in which the men of London and Stourbridge managed to improvise on the German models.

The next change in the style of English crystal occurred mainly as the result of an Act of Parliament. In 1745 an excise tax was imposed upon the materials used in glass-making, based on their weight. The glassmakers met the new situation in two ways: they reduced the quantity of lead used in their formulæ and they made their vessels lighter and more delicate in form.

The first effect of this was to diminish the richness of Ravenscroft's glass of lead: as has been aptly said, it now had the liquidity of water rather than of oil. Next, the use of thinner metal tended to hold up the development of deeper cutting, and in doing so it obviously put a greater emphasis on other means of decoration—engraving, enamelling and gilding. The curtain was thus lowered on English baroque, and it rose again on a home-made version of rococo—but a version which would scarcely be recognized anywhere but in England.

# 3. The Age of Decoration

Of these various new forms of decoration, the earliest was engraving, at first with the diamond-point, later with the cutter's wheel.

The point had been used on glass from classical times. A design could be scratched out in line, its shading or tone being provided by cross-hatching or perhaps stippling, as in engraving on copperplate. Outstanding work of this type was done in the seventeenth and eighteenth centuries by the Dutch engravers, notably Anna Roemers Visscher (1583–1651), one of the three engraver daughters of an Amsterdam merchant, also Frans Greenwood (1680–1761), a Rotterdam man of English extraction. In Elizabethan days the diamond point had been used on potash glass in England, perhaps by foreign workmen employed in Verzelini's workshops; but their work hardly bears comparison with that of the Dutch. The glass of the Ravenscroft era has very little of it to show, as one might expect from its nature, which, as we have seen, invited a different kind of decorating treatment.

By the turn of the century, however, the engravers had largely turned to the wheel. The art seems to have originated with Caspar Lehmann in Prague, but it spread to England from the Netherlands, presumably through the imported glass from that country in the early years of the century. The engravers sat at a revolving lathe, with its multitude of little copper discs. The surface was given its pattern by holding it against one of these wheels in a stream of water containing sand or some other abrasive, and turning the piece in the hands as required.

It was a tricky process, for the engraver's work was hidden from him by the wheel itself and also by the stream of water

*'Flowered' glasses:* (Above) *Wine, wheel engraved with grape and vine-leaf.* (Below) *Cordial, with garden flowers.* (Opposite) *Rummer, with hops and barley.* (All Victoria & Albert Museum.)

and sand. Great skill was also needed in the choice of the particular wheel used, and in this the Germans and the Dutch were especially adept.

Some of the earliest of the wheel engraving is to be found in heraldic work. There are some splendid glasses bearing the arms of William III, made about 1690, and others with those of Queen Anne, which would have dated from some twenty years later. They may have been made in England, but if they were, the engraving was done by a Dutchman. By 1735, however, wheel engraving was well established in London for we find Benjamin Payne advertising 'several curiosities engraved on glass' and 'the Arms of all the Royal family engraved on glass'.

English engravers—or perhaps at first Germans and Dutchmen working here—followed the currently fashionable formalism as shown in the imported *laub und bandelwerk* of the baroque. But the English engravers were no match for the Continentals in this style of decoration, and as though realizing this they moved over to a very English sort of naturalism: perhaps they took a hint from the Staffordshire potters, with their freely drawn roses on the delicious saltglazed stonewares and early creamwares.

## FLOWERED GLASSES

These 'flowered' glasses—a term first used by Jerome Johnson in an advertisement of 1742—did not necessarily show actual flowers. In the early days, 'flowered' glasses were much more likely to have grapes and vine-leaves for wine glasses, barley ears and hop vines for ales and apple trees for ciders. Some of the latter venture into politics. When an Act of 1763 imposed an excise duty on cider, the engravers—perhaps hoping that the Government would take note of the fact that this affected their own livelihood as well as the farmers'—would engrave on their glasses the slogan 'No excise' with a motif like a cider-barrel and cock.

When the full English garden appeared in glass engraving—it was happening at about the same time as flowers were being painted on porcelain—buyers could fill their cabinets with delicate engravings of roses (page 20), daffodils, sunflowers, daisies, carnations and the rest. There were also the usual birds, moths, bees and butterflies.

Engraving of this kind appeared not only on glasses, but also on decanters, tankards, goblets and bowls. The best of it was probably done before 1760: after that date there was an outbreak of all those swags and festoons, husks, geometrical borders, and other formal elements which heralded the Neo-classical style. Compared with the delightful native wood-notes of the 'flowered' glasses, this was dull, mechanical and repetitive stuff.

Much more engaging are two other classes of purely decorative engraving which flourished in the second half of the century. They both, in a sense, derived from motifs used happily on porcelain. One of them brought a light and skilful touch to bear on the romantic ruins and other classical subjects of contemporary ceramics; the other looked back to the *chinoiserie* of the mid-century. These are even more charming than the 'flowered glasses', and often appear in association with a lightly faceted stem. Mr W. A. Thorpe has suggested that their gaiety of mood and their delicate execution might indicate a Bristol origin for them.

JACOBITE GLASSES

The types of engraved glasses which seem to hold the attention of most collectors, however, are those which, like their cousins in pottery, commemorate some person, event or cause. Of the causes, that of the Jacobites probably accounts for as many of these glasses as all the others put together.

*Jacobite glasses:* (Above) *Rose and oak-leaf.* (Below) *Two buds on a 'Fiat' glass.* (Above right) *Portrait of the Young Pretender with 'Audentior Ibo' and rose emblems.* (Below right) *Williamite 'Immortal Memory' glass.* (All Victoria & Albert Museum.)

As is well known, when James II was driven from his throne in the 'Glorious Rebellion' of 1688, he left behind him supporters who formed themselves into groups which turned out (or failed to turn out) in favour of the ex-king's son, James Francis Edward, the Old Pretender, when he landed in Scotland in 1715 to claim his father's throne. In 1745 the Old Pretender's son, Prince Charles Edward (Bonnie Prince Charlie), appeared again on these shores to fight the Stuart cause, but although he penetrated into England as far as Derby, he fell back before the English troops. After defeat by the Duke of Cumberland at Culloden in 1746 he fled to the Continent.

It does not seem to be possible to date many Jacobite glasses to the years before Culloden. Soon after that very decisive event, however, they appeared in great numbers. The main group, called the 'Rose' glasses, show this flower—it is now generally agreed—as symbolizing the Crown. At first, with the rose itself, there appears a single rosebud, representing the Old Pretender. Later there is a second bud, for his son Prince Charles Edward.

There are also the well known 'Amen' glasses, on which this prayer is engraved in diamond point with a royal crown and cypher IR, usually with the figure 8—for James VIII of Scotland—and also the words of the Jacobite anthem. Only two dozen specimens are known, but there were some excellent forgeries of them in the 1930's.

The 'Fiat' glasses bear that word (meaning 'So be it') with various symbols, and there are portrait glasses having a likeness of the Young Pretender, often very crudely done. Other Jacobite mottoes include *Audentio Ibo* (I will go boldly), *Hic Vir Hic Est* (This is the man), *Reddas Incolumen* (May you return safely), *Redeat* (May he come back), and *Revirescit* (He is renewed).

The two-bud glasses (though not, it seems, the single-bud ones) may also carry further symbols. A star expressed hopes for the future of the House of Stuart, while an oak-leaf appears to be a recollection of the Boscobel Oak, in which Charles II hid when he escaped after the Battle of Worcester—this monarch wore an oak-leaf in his hat when he rode in triumph across London Bridge on his restoration in 1660. The 'Stricken Oak' symbolizes the unlucky fate of the House, and sometimes shows a young sapling and the inscription *Revirescit.*

The compass and the forget-me-not appear as a remembrance of past times, apparently well after the death of Prince Charles Edward. There are also a great many other late glasses with combinations of flowers and insects. In these so-called 'decay-of-the-movement' glasses specialist collectors find symbols of the decline of hopes for the cause.

*Large Masonic punch rummer, two coaching glasses* (Delomosne & Son) *and inscribed wine.* (Victoria & Albert Museum.)

### WILLIAMITE GLASSES

Less romantic in origin, but hardly less interesting historically are the 'Williamite' glasses, favoured by supporters of 'The glorious pious and immortal memory of the great and good King William, who freed us from Pope and popery, knavery and slavery, brass money and wooden shoes': in fact, by the opponents of everything which they felt the Stuart cause represented. The glasses often commemorate the Battle of the Boyne or show a portrait of King William, either as a bust or as full figure on horseback—the latter familiar to collectors of blue-dash chargers in delftware.*

But in fact, although commemorating a monarch of the seventeenth century, most of the 'Williamite' glasses actually date from the late eighteenth or early nineteenth centuries. This does not mean they are necessarily forgeries; it is due to the course taken by politics. At first the 'Williamite' glasses were a reply to Jacobite dreams of restoration to the throne when that still seemed possible; but as time went on, and the Jacobite dream faded, the Williamite cause drew increased strength from the anti-popery agitations arising in protest against the emancipation of the Roman Catholics.

### COMMEMORATIVE AND OTHER ENGRAVING

Contemporary events are celebrated by the engravers mainly through persons engaged in them. Frederick the Great, hero of the Seven Years War, and an ally of England against France, is a favourite here as he is in pottery. One glass shows the hapless Admiral Byng in full dress uniform

* See *Delftware* in this series.

*Punchbowl cut and engraved with hunting scene, dated 1756.* (Victoria & Albert Museum.)

*Newcastle rummer, with engraved view of the Tyne bridge.* (Laing Art Gallery, Newcastle-upon-Tyne.)

hanging from a gallows—although in fact this person was shot. He is the officer to whom Voltaire was referring when he remarked that every now and then the English shot another admiral 'to encourage the others'.

The Peninsular, Napoleonic and other campaigns are commemorated, and portraits of Nelson, Wellington and various naval commanders appear. There are also regimental glasses, inscribed with insignia. The fine lines of ships' rigging lent themselves nicely to engraving, as is shown by much-admired series of frigates and the Bristol privateers.

The union of Great Britain and Ireland is commemorated, also the opening of the Wearmouth Bridge at Sunderland, so ubiquitous on pottery. Our picture shows not the Wearmouth but the High Level bridge over the Tyne at Newcastle, on local glass.

As might be expected of the eighteenth and early nineteenth centuries, sporting scenes were highly popular, and covered not only fox-hunting, but steeplechasing, fishing, shooting, cock-fighting, coursing, stag-hunting and horse racing. Travel had its commemorations in the form of the well-known coaching glasses; there are others for inns, railways and canals.

Trades have their glasses, decorated with 'arms' of the Turners, Stationers, Weavers, Butchers, Swordmakers, and very understandably wishing themselves success and prosperity. Private affairs also have their place, from birth and christening to betrothal, coming of age and even death. People also remembered on glass their houses, farms, windmills, castles, as well as their pet animals, friends and relations and also their many convivial occasions.

A caveat must once again be entered about forgeries, which are particularly rife in the field of engraved commemorative glass. Sometimes the glasses themselves are of modern make, in which case the connoisseur's instinct for spurious metal, shape and making must come into play. In other cases, the glasses are genuine enough but the engraving has been added later—perhaps long enough ago by now to have acquired the appearance of age. Fortunately much of this work is crudely conceived and executed, and Mr Thorpe especially recommends watching the broad strokes in letter inscriptions, where small chips appear more often in false than in genuine work. Of personages, Dean Swift,

(Left to right) *Privateer or Frigate glass, 'King of Prussia' wine, and cordial painted in enamels by the Beilbys of Newcastle-upon-Tyne.* (All Victoria & Albert Museum.)

Admiral Byng, the Young Pretender, John Wesley, Nelson and especially William III, have been brought to life again, and glasses commemorating them should be treated with due circumspection.

### 'TEAR' TO 'AIR-TWIST'

English crystal glass of lead, when thick enough, can acquire bubbles without any help, in fact it very much enjoys doing so. This seeming fault was turned into a decorative virtue by gaffers even in Ravenscroft's day. They could control a bubble in such a way as to form a 'tear' in the stems of glasses, so helping to entrap light in the rich new metal.

With the drawn-stem type of glass it was easy enough to do. A depression was made in the top of the stem and covered with another blob of glass; the air expanded as it heated, and when the stem was drawn out into a bowl, the bubble took upon itself the typical pear shape.

From this it was not many steps to the 'air-twist' as seen on page 39. The gaffer could make several holes in his gather by thrusting it into a shaped mould; he could then seal the ends with another blob of glass and draw the whole gather out long and thin, twisting it to his fancy. Compound twists could be made up by bringing together two or more lengths of twisted rod. In their brighter and more silvery forms, these 'air-twists' have been misleadingly described as 'mercury-twists', but in fact it is technically impossible to combine mercury with molten glass.

### 'ENAMEL-TWISTS'

The 'air-twist' contained nothing but air; the 'enamel-twist' which followed and superseded it contained opaque white or coloured glass giving a fascinating variety of colourful spirals.

Here the glassmaker produced something like the Venetian *latticinio*, using a mould with grooves round it. In these he arranged opaque, white or coloured glass in fine canes which projected over the top like a palisade. Between these rods he thrust a gather of clear crystal so that the canes adhered to the hot surface of the glass. The rods were then embedded firmly into the crystal by 'marvering', i.e. rolling up and down on the gaffer's marver, or iron table. Afterwards the whole 'paraison' was drawn out between two men, twisting as they pulled away from each other and thus making a long slender rope of glass containing white or coloured spirals.

By combining different shapes, filigree threads, ribbons, etc., and multiplying the process, the gaffer could build up a great variety of effects in the way of lace or cable patterns, mixing both shapes and colours in endless spirals. Red, blue and green opaque glass was used, also, more rarely, lavender, yellow and black. Occasionally use was made of coloured crystal glass, as distinct from opaque and 'enamel'.

The earliest dated opaque-twist glass is of the year 1747. As already noted, this method of decoration was greatly encouraged by the excise tax of 1745, with its inhibiting effect on the use of glass in bulk and its exemption from excise duties of all 'enamel' glass. Thirty years later, however, another excise tax not only doubled the duty on crystal but now imposed a heavy impost on 'enamel' glass. After this the opaque-twist faded out of the picture almost entirely.

*High shoulder label decanter, with enamel painting in blue and white by Beilbys of Newcastle-upon-Tyne.* c. *1770.* (Victoria & Albert Museum.)

*Cut-glass jug.*
(Delomosne & Son.)

ENAMEL PAINTING

Of the glasses which have been 'enamelled' by painting on their surfaces, the most famous are those made by the Beilby family, of Newcastle-upon-Tyne.

Their products fall into several distinct classes. The 'white' family includes ales and small wines with straight-sided or ogee bowls which may have the same kinds of engraving as we have already been discussing—flowers, vine leaves, hops and barley and sometimes birds. Others have pleasant little rustic subjects—scenes of fishing, shooting, skating, etc., which are strongly reminiscent of the engraving of Thomas Bewick who, in fact, was apprenticed to the Beilbys. Decanters show vine and grape motifs in rococo panels (page 27) and also the subjects in the romantic tradition with the classical ruins, obelisks and *chinoiserie* which have been noted among the engraved glasses.

In colours there are rare landscapes, but quite a number of heraldic pieces. These include goblets, decanters, firing glasses, etc., with heraldic motifs which are sometimes quite fictitious, set up in the usual rococo scrollwork. A few are signed 'Beilby', and according to a memoir left by Bewick they are the work of William Beilby's son and daughter, William and Mary, in their efforts to help the family out of financial disaster.

CUT-GLASS

For many people, the term crystal or flint glass means, simply and exclusively, cut-glass.

There are good reasons for this. Glass of lead, soft and rich in texture, heavy and liquid in behaviour, scarcely needs the aid of such ornament as engraving gives—except, as we have seen, when it has been 'starved' by penal taxation. No doubt this was the reason why the Dutch and Germans were usually our masters with the diamond point or the engraving wheel. Their thin potash glass was nothing without decoration of this kind.

Cutting deeply or shallowly with the metal wheel in mainly geometrical designs was a process which, by entrapping light throughout its mass, brought out the full brilliance of the glass. In the finest period of cut-glass—say between 1760 and the over-elaboration which set in about 1790—there was a well-nigh perfect balance between form and decoration. Mr Thorpe has aptly said of this work that the two go so well together that we ought always to give the term cut-glass its hyphen. It is hardly surprising that during its best period English cut crystal was the first English glass to excite the envy of the Continental gaffers, and is the only type which has ever really made its mark in other countries.

If you visit that typical Stourbridge factory already mentioned, you will find that the cutters are still using much the same methods as did their predecessors in the eighteenth century. You may see a few new tools or methods of polishing, but basically the procedure is the same. A pattern is marked out on the glass with red lead-paint as a guide to the cutter, who then roughs out the work with a soft-iron wheel which is either flat, rounded or mitred (V-shaped), according to the cut desired. The cutting is done by holding the glass against the wheel under a stream of water and sand. This coarse finish is then refined with a sandstone wheel using water only. Afterwards the rest of the design is cut in with smaller wheels. The job, of course, calls for a high degree of personal skill of hand and eye.

*Cut-glass butter-dish.*
(Delomosne & Son.)

*Fruit bowls, showing* (above) *strawberry diamond cutting and* (opposite) *hollow diamonds with fan escallop edging.* c. *1810.* (Both Victoria & Albert Museum.)

The original brilliance of the glass then has to be restored by polishing. This was once done by using wheels of cork or wood fed with some soft abrasive like putty powder or rouge. The same method is still used today for pieces of the best quality, but less valuable objects are usually given a bath in acid.

Basically all cuts are founded upon what can be done with wheels whose edges are flat, rounded or mitred. This last can be used either to make a complete mitre, or, by applying only one side and the point on a rounded surface, an edge flute or slice. The flat cutting was done with either a flat-edged wheel or a slightly rounded one, but the mitre cut received its full development in the deep cutting, especially with the diamond, in the heyday of Anglo-Irish work. One has only to examine a piece to see the way designs were built up from parallel grooves intersecting with others at right angles. The mitre was also used for prismatic cutting. Whereas most cutting is made up of straight lines, or of straight scoopings-out of glass, the incised line, perhaps the most difficult of all, calls for turning the pieces in one's hand across the wheel.

At first the cutting was used in the most tentative and restrained way. The keen hostess's eye of Lady Grizell Baillie, when she ventured from her home in Scotland into London society (see also page 50), notes in her diary for 1727 that Lord Carlisle had a dessert-set with 'a high scallop'd glass in the middle'. This was no doubt something like the sweetmeat glass shown on page 51. A few years later at Lord Mountjoy's, she writes of 'cornered brim'd glasses', meaning much the same thing.

EARLY SHALLOW CUTTING

This was the main form of early cutting, and it is a delightful one. For surface decoration the work was quite shallow—such flat cutting, as it is called, is well seen in the cruet bottle shown on page 53. There were flat, vertical flutes, sometimes found on a shouldered stem, rounded flutes on bowls, triangular facets, diamonds, and long hexagons. A good deal of cutting is found around the feet, also many incised and sliced motifs—zigzag circuits, lunar slices, festoons, arches, even relief triangles and diamonds.

Some of the scalloping was in the form of arch and angle, or the rims might be regularly undulating or in zigzags. Feet were also scalloped out in arcs or straight lines, giving polygonal forms.

Then came the Act of 1745, with its inhibiting effect upon the weight of metal—and therefore on the extension of the deeper cutting which, had the gaffer not been faced with thinner walls, would obviously have been the next line of development. Historians have called this era, say 1746 to 1780, the 'Arrest' Period, when cutting—except for articles where cost was not in question, e.g. candlesticks, sweetmeats, chandeliers—took second place to the forms of decoration we have been looking at in the preceding pages.

All the same, some excellent cutting was done in this period. The early motifs were developed in greater variety, giving effects like scale-pattern on the necks of bottles or the 'arch and sprig' between the stem and the lower part of a bowl. Fluting developed on necks and as 'comb fluting' around the bases of decanters and on bowls and lids. Stem-faceting was a special feature of the cutting of the period and it gives us some of the most attractive of all the drinking glasses and candlesticks (see page 59). There were long diamonds, sometimes 'hooked', and long hexagons; there were sliced motifs on feet; while with the coming of the rococo much curved scalloping was found on epergnes, girandoles and chandeliers. Further development also took place in the relief diamond, which was to become one of the basic motifs in the next period.

### ANGLO-IRISH DEEP CUTTING

This began around the years 1777–80, when two events occurred which were to change the whole future of crystal glass. In 1777–9, as already noted, the excise tax of 1745 was doubled. In the following year, Ireland, where there was no excise duty, was granted free trade, which meant that whereas there had hitherto (since 1745) been a total prohibition on her sending glass to any country whatever, she could now export freely.

*Covered jug with pineapple pattern.* c. 1725. (Victoria & Albert Museum.)

At once the little Irish glass industry found it profitable to buy materials from England and engage in a thriving export trade to the newly liberated United States, the West Indies and the Continent of Europe. English glassmakers from Stourbridge and other centres had long been established in Ireland, mainly as refugees from the English excise duty: they were now joined by another and much larger wave of immigrants from England and also from Germany.

At this date it is extremely difficult, lacking a mark, to distinguish the product of one Irish factory from another. They all used each other's 'cullet' waste, so that their material as well as their workmanship is almost indistinguishable. There are stylistic differences by which connoisseurs place pieces with one factory or another, but usually they will not go much further than to say that a specimen is 'characteristic' of Cork, Waterford, Dublin, etc. The legend that Waterford glass is peculiar for its blue tinge is, one has to say, only a legend, for this colour was liable to occur anywhere when there was an excess of cobalt or some other dye in the metal.

In styles and motifs the Irish cutters took over the existing English ones and added others particularly suited to deep cutting. Perhaps the most outstanding of these was the development of the relief diamond, which could be used as a field or diaper. At first there were large double-cut diamonds, then, towards the end of the century, fields of small diamonds. This eventually produced the famous 'strawberry diamond' (see page 30), a combination of the double-cut diamond with a field of small relief diamonds. When it has a central star it is called the 'hobnail' pattern. By about 1810 this had been introduced into England, where it became one of the chief features of Regency glass. The Anglo-Irish era also saw greatly extended use of the flute, especially the pillared variety.

Prismatic step cutting also had a great upsurge at this time, and was popular because it could be adapted to so many forms. The herringbone fringe, either upright or sloping, appears in the early nineteenth century, also trefoil scalloping and—especially at Waterford—fan-cut edges.

The early shallow sprig, perhaps done by the engraver, was now cut deeply into a fan or star. This latter, either on its own or in combination with other motifs, could range from the simple six-point to the spectacular Brunswick star, which called for no fewer than twenty-four cuts; and even this could be developed into more complicated forms.

## MOULDED AND BLOWN-MOULDED GLASS

Shaping glass vessels in a mould, either by blowing or pouring the metal into it, is something one tends nowadays to associate with nineteenth-century imitations of cut-glass. But the process has a respectable and in fact very ancient history, going back into the dim beginnings of glassmaking.

English crystal of the eighteenth century often made use of the mould to give preliminary shaping and a surface pattern. Where a piece was of such a shape that it could not be withdrawn from the mould after blowing, use was made of a two- or three-part mould which could be taken apart.

Many types of sweetmeats were made in this way, also decanters, on which the maker's name, for example Penrose of Waterford, could be impressed. Vertical ribbing was given to wine-glass bowls and a wrythen or twisted effect could be obtained by twisting the body as it was withdrawn

*Wines with moulded and cut decoration. $4\frac{3}{4}$ and $4\frac{1}{2}$ in.* c. *1830.* (Victoria & Albert Museum.)

from the mould. From about the end of the century, flat-ware such as dishes, plates, salts and the like were pressed in moulds. These were the precursors of the great flood of blown-moulded glass made in the early nineteenth century for the prospering middle and lower classes. The process was taken to even more spectacular lengths by the glassmen in the United States.

Much of this work followed the designs of the cut-glass with which it competed, and by making available to the general what had hitherto been the preserve of the particular it greatly undermined the reputation of cutting. One result was an outbreak of extravagant cutting, the other was a revival of interest in the simple blown forms of Venice.

Nevertheless, in the early days of this moulding the glass was still English crystal of the old kind, and much of it used motifs which it had been impossible to achieve with the earlier methods. Such wares have for some time now been the quarry of a new race of collectors.

*Wine with foliate engraving and stem cut with long diamonds. Perhaps the original 'champagne' shape.* (Victoria & Albert Museum.)

# 4. The Wares

### DRINKING GLASSES

Something must now be said about the different kinds of wares made in English crystal glass. If one starts with drinking glasses it is not so much from any personal predilection as that they constitute the largest single class of items and perhaps offer us the greatest variety of form and decoration. The problem is how to present anything like a coherent account of them in so small a book.

One would like to begin by talking of their uses, but authorities have sometimes been over-eager to award particular kinds of glasses to particular drinks. Georgian wine glasses, for example, come in many shapes—they will be described later—and it is sometimes difficult to distinguish them from ales. The flute-shaped glass, for example, has traditionally been associated with malted drinks, but it is sometimes engraved with the fruiting vine pattern, which seems to elect it as a wine.

Glasses with a wide round bowl are generally associated with champagne; but Disraeli was astonished to find himself offered 'The Boy' in one of these. Some of the alleged champagnes, in fact, have an everted or out-turned rim which makes them practically impossible to drink from without soaking one's shirtfront: this surely points to their being sweetmeats. But there *are* named champagnes in the early advertisements, and they appear to have looked like the glass on page 36.

The rummer is another glass which has its legends. A short-stemmed version of the goblet, with a round or bucket-shaped bowl, it is said to have been used for grog, or hot rum and water. But in Gayton's *Pleasant Notes* there is mention of a 'lusty rummer of Rhenish'. This and other evidence suggests that what was first called the rummer in

*Early eighteenth-century glass shapes:* (Left to right) *Anglo-Venetian style wine with long inverted baluster.* c. *1710. 7½ in. German thistle bowl on English mushroom balustroid knop.* c. *1710. 8 in. Anglo-Venetian round funnel bowl on a German (Silesian) four-shouldered stem with bosses.* c. *1710. 6⅜ in. 'Light baluster' wine with bell bowl and English engraving in the German baroque style.* c. *1730. 6½ in.*

this country was originally the *roemer*, a German name for what was then known as a 'Roman' glass with 'prunts' on the stem. It was apparently used here for 'Rhenish' wine and then made prolifically in this country in the late Ravenscroft era: you can see its descendants on the tables of the Rhineland today. In later forms it dropped the prunts, took up other forms like the bucket bowl (page 39), and sometimes expanded itself into a large bowl for rum punch.

### DRAMS AND 'DECEPTIVES'

Some glasses suggest their uses by their capacities. The Georgian dram, for example, was obviously used for spirits, while the cordials, with their tiny bowls perched upon long stems, could only have been for what we now know as liqueurs. There are fluted versions of these, known as ratafia glasses, after a concoction of brandy and other ingredients which was popular in that day among ladies. They have also been called surfeit glasses, after another and more potent of these brews offered after a Georgian meal—at which, it seems, a surfeit was almost inevitable.

Also easily identifiable are the toastmaster, 'chairman', or

(Left to right) *'Ratafia' glass with drawn enamel twists stem and flowered engraving.* c. *1755. 7¼ in. Wine with bell bowl, cut with long diamond facets, terrace and slice cutting on foot.* c. *1740. 7½ in. Goblet with bucket bowl painted in enamels with air-twist stem.* c. *1765. 6⅞ in. Firing glass with Masonic emblems painted in coloured enamels.* c. *1765. 3⅛ in.*

'deceptive' glasses, in which the bowl was so made that while it looked full of liquor it was actually much more full of glass. This helped the Georgian toastmaster or chairman (otherwise the host) through the many toasts he had to give and respond to in the course of a long and rumbustious Georgian evening. These are not to be confused, however, with the toasting glass, which has so slender a stem that it could be—and on appropriate occasions was—snapped between the fingers and tossed away, so that no lesser lady or monarch could be toasted in it. Not surprisingly, few of these have survived.

STEM, BOWL AND FOOT

The opposite of the toasting glass so far as strength and endurance is concerned is the 'firing' glass (page 42). This is a short-stemmed piece having so thick a foot that it can be thumped on the table in answer to a toast. At a dinner party of any size the noise must have sounded something like a volley of pistol shots.

It is, however, by their parts that drinking glasses are best classified, that is to say, by the shape and type of stem, bowl and foot. Some were made in three separate pieces, others only in two, the bowl being drawn out to make the stem. But the basic classification now in common use seems to be, first, by the stem, then by the variations in bowl and foot. In this way, one can find a home for any kind of glass, whatever its shape.

To take stems first, English crystal, as we have seen, started with the baluster, which gave its whole name to the immediately post-Ravenscroft era. To the superficial glance, these balusters, with their simple forms and virtual absence of decoration, seem to have no attraction beyond the splendour of their metal. But in fact there is endless variety in the form of the stems, and in the felicity or otherwise in which they combine with bowl and foot. This is perhaps why they have excited glass connoisseurs for many years.

The baluster, as one might expect, was not allowed to remain undeveloped, and there is a whole race of glasses which have acquired the name 'balustroid' to indicate their kinship with the purer form. There are 'inverted' balusters; there are glasses where the knop is wide and angular, annulated or ringed, dropped or cushioned; the bowl may also take the form of an acorn, a cylinder, a mushroom or an oval. Most often seen on these glasses, however, is the round funnel bowl, although conical, waisted and other types are also found. The well-known 'Kitcat' glasses, named after those seen in paintings of members of that club, are of the balustroid type.

There is also a distinctive race from Newcastle called 'light balusters': these were much in demand by the Dutch for their engraving, and many were exported to that country for this purpose.

It is interesting to speculate what would have happened to English glasses had there not now appeared in this country the German glasses already mentioned (see page 38). The shouldered or 'Silesian' stem was the most conspicuous feature of these glasses. Its earliest form was a four-sided pedestal, afterwards developing six or even eight sides, perhaps with vertical twisting and reeding. The shoulders could be sloping or vertically adorned with bosses. As with the previous group, the bowl most often seen was the round funnel, although again, conical, waisted and other types are found.

The largest groups of stems, however, are those in glasses of two-piece construction where the stem is drawn out to make a bowl and the foot added. The glasses made in this way were economical in labour, and therefore cheap, so they became the ordinary commerce of tavern and home. Again, however, there is a great variety in bowl and foot shape, and this class includes a great many of the dram glasses and firing glasses, also the famous 'Hogarth' glasses, so named because of their appearance in several of that artist's paintings and engravings. Many bear engravings of the 'flowered' sort, the taller flutes having hops and barley, the wine shapes the fruiting vine.

*A group of 'pub wines' bought in various places at prices from ten to twenty-five shillings each.*

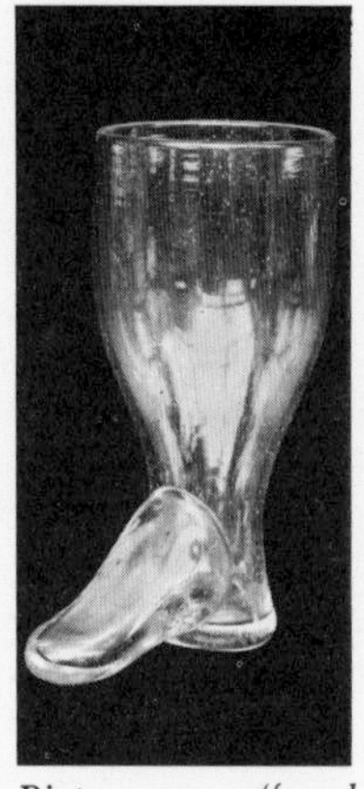

*Pint measure ('yard of ale'). 36½ in. long. Shoe drinking cup.* (Both British Museum.) *Toddy lifter and firing glass with arms of H.R.H. Prince Augustus, Duke of Sussex. Coaching or stirrup cup.* (Victoria & Albert Museum.)

Next among the stems come the air, incised and enamel twists, also the composites: these again can be sub-divided into types of twists. A smallish group has a hollow stem with or without knops, perhaps designed to save weight after the Act of 1745.

Glasses with faceted stems obviously belong to the cut-glass family, and very pleasant members of it they are. They do not appear much before 1760 and seem to have had their heyday between 1780 and 1810. Sometimes the foot is also decorated with scalloping or rose cutting—alternate arch and point—round the rim. There may be fluting at the join of the bowl and stem, and sometimes at the point where the stem meets the foot.

Finally, there are the glasses with short stems or none at all. In this stunted but nevertheless most engaging class are many of the dwarf ales (for the 'stingo' of the day), the drams, and some of the wines and rummers.

Bowls may have the shapes of bells, buckets, cups, trumpets, thistles, round funnels; they may be conical, waisted, ogee, hexagonal or octagonal. These shapes may themselves be modified in various ways, especially at the lip or the base; or they may start life as an ogee and have a cup or a bucket on top.

Alongside the Silesian stem, the German glasses which came in with the German kings had added to the Italianate forms of the Greene and Ravenscroft eras several new bowl shapes, notably the bell, the thistle, the trumpet and various waisted types. As the Silesian stem disappeared from drinking glasses, these bowl forms adapted themselves in the most interesting ways to the existing English balustroid stems.

They also merged with foot forms like the plain conical, the folded (where the glass has been turned under the edge for strength), the domed (in which the foot has a high instep which may also be terraced), the ringed and the oversewn. Some other foot forms showed bases which were flanged or shaped like a beehive or a pedestal.

*Decanters:* (Left to right) *Cut all over with diamond facets, pyramid stopper cut in diamonds.* c. 1755. *12 in. High-shouldered type with cut and engraved decoration, disc stopper with lunar cutting.* c. *1755. 11¼ in. Low-shouldered 'label' type with disc stopper. Barrel type with ringed neck and mushroom stopper.*

All these elements, once absorbed by the native gaffer and transformed by his skill and good taste, gave us in the drinking glasses of the eighteenth century some of the most coherent and beautiful of glass forms.

BOTTLES AND DECANTERS

Today most of us know the difference between a bottle and a decanter but it was not always so obvious. The earliest decanters were simply serving bottles, in which wine drawn from a barrel was taken to the table. They took the shape of the ordinary bottles of the day, at first that very basic form, the globe surmounted by a long-shafted neck. Ravenscroft advertised them, complete with stoppers, ribbed 'all over nipt diamond waies', at four shillings a time—something to stagger the imagination of today's collectors. Some examples of his 'extraordinary work' is seen on such bottles. Forty years later came the 'onion', a squat type with a shorter neck, sometimes with a handle and a pinched lip for pouring.

From here on, bottle and decanter go their separate

ways, for we have reached the age of port and other heavy wines which were matured in the bottle. The wine bottle elongated itself so that it could lie flat in the bin, the wine itself keeping the cork moist and therefore excluding air. From this moment it became necessary to have another vessel into which one could pour wine which had been binned for some time and had thus acquired a sediment or crust which was not required in the glass.

Thus the bin bottle, stowed away in the dark cellar, remained in bottle-green glass, while the serving bottle, conspicuous on the table, moved up into crystal: and the alchemists were all ready with their Latin word *decanthare* (from *canthus*, an edge), i.e. to tilt a vessel in such a way as to pour its contents over an 'edge' and separate a liquid from a precipitate. By 1755 Johnson had defined a decanter in his dictionary as a vessel made for receiving liquor clear from the lees.

Left to itself, the decanter lengthened its neck again, straightened its inward sloping sides, sometimes acquired a handle; and might, instead of a stopper, have a ring on its neck over which was tied a cover of parchment. It tended to have a high 'kick' in its foot to help in the primitive annealing or cooling process used before the invention of a tunnel for this purpose.

There is still a 'bottle' quality about this shape; but in the next stage it parted company from its mate altogether and became a balloon, not unlike the original shaft and globe. This was much favoured by the Jacobites. About 1735 it finally dropped the string ring and again had its neck ground out for a stopper.

In these early decades of the eighteenth century there appeared the mallet-shape, with octagonal or hexagonal sides, which could be vertical or slightly inward sloping, and with shoulders nearly at right angles. It might also have a ball-finialled stopper. A refinement on this was the quatrefoil or cruciform decanter, with four lobes reaching out to form a cross.

SHORT AND TALL SHOULDERS

By the middle of the eighteenth century, and continuing in use until its end, the basic design was the shouldered decanter. This feature varied in height. The type with the shorter shoulder was the first to be cut, usually with flat diamonds, and would have a spire finial stopper, cut at the same time as the decanter.

The tall-shouldered decanter with outward sloping body came in about 1740–50. Its shape is shown on page 27. The missing stopper would perhaps have been a plain spire finial. It was on this type that there first appeared engraved inscriptions naming the liquors they were to contain: Port, Claret, Mountain and the rest. They were called 'label decanters', but somewhere after 1770 they seem to have been overtaken by the craze for heavy cutting, and the labelling was done by hanging round the bottle necks the well-known wine labels or bottle tickets of silver, enamel, Sheffield plate and other materials.

*Decanter styles:* (Above) *Diamond and flute cutting with mushroom knop to match.* (Right) *Waterford engraved type with triple rings and lozenge knop.* (Both Victoria & Albert Museum.) (Opposite) *Barrel shape with diamond cutting and gilt banding.* (Delomosne & Son.)

The short-shouldered decanter seems to have slipped by easy stages into the taper, an elegant shape with the shoulder falling away to a mere slope, usually very lightly cut with flutings, festooning and stars. The finial stopper might at first have a flat vertical disc or target finial but later the taper appeared with the flat vertical lozenge or pear shape.

The barrel-shaped decanter appeared about 1775 and had a long life, extending through the Anglo-Irish period down to Victorian days. It had the heaviest cutting of all, making a great show of relief diamonds, and, for the first time, rings appeared round the neck, cut in various styles, and often crowned by the mushroom stopper characteristic of Waterford. It was followed by the cylinder decanter, again with heavy cutting, sometimes with inch-wide vertical flutes running the whole way up the body. It is an unglassy type, and the more successful decanters which followed look back for inspiration to their predecessors.

STOPPER STYLES

Finials of stoppers have been mentioned, and they are worth study to make sure they belong to the decanters they sit in. Earliest is the uncut spire finial, later pear-shaped, and found with the early short and long-shouldered decanters. When the latter acquired facets, or lightly hollowed diamonds, the stopper followed suit. Sometimes there was a ball knop between finial and stopper. Following it, on the tall shoulders, came the flat vertical disc: it might have a notched edge or cut sides. The taper decanter called for this in a slenderer, lozenge-shaped form.

With the barrel, as noted above, came the mushroom, often cut or moulded in ridges, but after 1790 with cutting matching that on the vessel. The barrel might also have the target stopper, which was an upright disc with a large boss in the middle and cut or moulded ridges on the edges. There were also flat finials in the shape of hearts or clover-leaves, while the later cylindrical decanters often had a tall and very weighty pinnacle finial.

'Squares' were made in the second half of the eighteenth century, for rough handling in taverns and coaches. Some were blown-moulded, with flat cutting at first and then convex diamonds. They often bore an owner's cypher gilded or engraved, and the smaller sizes appeared in sets in travelling cases. They usually had stoppers with a faceted ball finial. An unusual shape which well indicates its purpose is the Rodney, or ship's decanter, with a very wide bottom: a vessel would have had to capsize before the Rodney lost its contents.

### TOILET BOTTLES

No very loud songs have been sung in praise of the many small toilet bottles which crystal glass has given us. This may be because so many of them have silver, gold or copper mounts and have thus been placed in a sort of never-never land where they tend to be neglected both by specialist collectors of silver and of glass.

But they are worth looking at, and in an age when one must often be restricted by room, even more worth while collecting. It may be necessary to remind oneself that the full splendour of cut-glass occurred in the same age which saw the blossoming

(Left) *Silver-mounted scent bottle.* (Delomosne & Son.) (Opposite above) *Apsley Pellatt glass 'sulphide' cameo.* (Victoria & Albert Museum.) (Opposite below) *Condiment bottles and stand, cut-glass ink-bottles and stand.* (Eric Delieb.)

of the craft of Sheffield plate. If you can afford it, it seems worth doing a little trespassing in the field of both silver and plate collector.

The smelling bottle—the name reflects an older usage—was an intimate piece of property, so, whatever the medium, it called for fine craftsmanship and decorative skill. In crystal glass many appear from their size to have been designed for the table rather than the pocket or the reticule. But in both sorts one sees the transition from the shallow cutting of the early days to the deep diamonds of the Anglo-Irish era.

Apart from the metal mounts—which will often give you a date—there are other kinds of additions which for some people hold a new interest and for others merely serve as a

distraction from the noble simplicity of crystal itself. Of such are the small jasper-ware cameos* which Wedgwood sold to the glassmakers for mounting upon their bottles; also the silver 'sulphides' made by Apsley Pellatt, by means of which a portrait of frosted glass was imbedded in the pure crystal.

DESSERT GLASSES

Many kinds of dessert glasses are to be found in English crystal. In the eighteenth century this piece was used not only for fruit, but for all the many delectabilities offered at social gatherings or towards the end of the Georgian meal—jellies, trifles, ice-creams, syllabubs, bergamot chips, sugar plums, biscuits, cakes, chocolates, bonbons, comfits, candies, etc.

These pleasant commodities, as will be seen, fall into two classes, the 'wet' and the 'dry'. As in the case of the alleged champagnes, however, commentators have tended, I think, to carry classification too far: for example, those glasses which stand upon a tall stem or pedestal, with wide bowls and an everted rim (page 51), are sometimes said to be for 'wet' things like custards and creams, sometimes for 'dry' items such as orange chips.

In trying to solve this problem it may be worth ignoring the stems and concentrating on the bowls. The plain rims and double ogee bowls obviously seem to lend themselves to sundaes and things of that kind, especially to syllabubs. The latter was an interesting drink made by mixing, say, a quart of cream with a pint of sack (sherry), flavouring it with lemon, and whisking it up. One filled the lower part of the bowl with some sweetened claret, sack or white wine, then dropped the creamy froth into the cup-shaped part of the bowl, and drank the former through the latter, as with 'Gaelic' coffee.

But Lady Grizell's 'cornered brim'd glasses', or, going back a little, those which have the hyaloplastic loopings of the baroque period, might seem more suitable for the bon-

*See *Wedgwood Jasper Ware* in this series.

*Eighteenth century sweetmeat glasses:* (Left) *With everted rim and Silesian stem.* (Centre and right) *'Cornered brim'd'* (*see page 50*). (All Victoria & Albert Museum.)

bon, the comfit, and other things which may be picked up with the fingers; so too, possibly, the smaller bowls and boats without stands, or with only rudimentary ones. The jellies and custard glasses, however, are another matter. They have the same shapes today, and can easily be recognized (page 52).

So far as styles are concerned, those with tall stems follow the normal progression. They appeared first in the baluster age with squat, bell-shaped or double ogee bowl, usually quite plain. From about 1700, however, they began to acquire vertical ribbing or purling; this led to the Silesian stem, which lingered on in dessert glasses much longer than in drinking vessels. One wonders if the reason was that eighteenth-century ladies were more conservative than men.

We have already noted how Lady Grizell Baillie, that perspicacious housewife, showed a special interest in Lord

*Custard or jelly glasses and stand.* (Victoria & Albert Museum.)

Mountjoy's 'cornered brim'd glasses' set out for dessert. Collectors will find it well worth their while plunging into her fascinating *Household Book*, which covers the years 1692 to 1733. There she records all kinds of interesting and sometimes astonishing items; her 'standing orders' to her staff suggest that she thought of them as total imbeciles. When she went out she faithfully noted every small detail of the food and drink offered her, as well as the type of glass or china on which it was served. On one December evening at the house of Lord Carlisle she took the trouble to make a ground plan of the 'deseart'. This is given below.

> Deseart: 9 all on guilt cornered salvers, low feet; midle, with one row glass salvers with half inch broad brims with franch plumb, Apricoks, fruts dry, Almond bisket and Ratafia. 8 in all, and wafers put in betwixt them, a salver above that w$^{t}$ 4 frute jellys and wet sweatmeats, with covers, and betwixt them high glasses, white confits on the top, a scolloped glass cornered brim.
>
> 2 ends bottom row, Jelly harts horn and limon and ratafia cream, a salver on top with the same cornered brimd glasses as in the midle.
>
> 2 sids 1st row, Aples in sawcers and frensh figs and plumbs, the last pistashe nuts on one and aples in cyrop in the other, the same cornerd brimd glasses as the rest, the 4 corners, 2 slist oranges and 2 almonds and resins, in glass broad cream bowls.

### SALVERS AND STANDS

Lady Grizell mentions salvers: with all these dessert glasses to display, several kinds of stands and salvers were used, especially at a ball or 'rout' when they were pyramided on side-tables. Three or four salvers of diminishing sizes would be stood one upon another with a 'top' or 'orange' glass on the highest—this was a footed glass like those discussed above. The other glasses would be displayed on the various tiers, some of which revolved on their pedestals.

Stemmed salvers would also be used for carrying wine around at receptions. The earliest of these look like Venetian *tazzi*, with hollow stems, but there soon appeared the more solid baluster. Later the Silesian stem was almost usual. In fact, throughout the century it seemed to recur whenever people wanted to put on dog. Perhaps a good reason for having it on salvers was that the ribbed sides gave your serving man a better grip on the stem. In cutting days there might have been a scalloped brim with geometrical work on the under surface.

For the dinner table, as a show piece, there was the centre stand. These were large *tazzi* with tall stems, and a knop from which radiated various branches, hooked at their ends to carry glass baskets. Later, these elaborated themselves into epergnes, which in their full splendour would have

(Left to right) *Mallet-shaped cruet bottle cut with shallow diamonds, printies, etc.* c. *1730–40. 5 in. Creamer with diamond cutting.* c. *1800–10. $3\frac{1}{4}$ in. Butter-dish.* c. *1800–1810. $5\frac{7}{8}$ in.* (All Victoria & Albert Museum.)

curved, faceted or notched branches held in silver or gilt fittings from the stem. These might be facet-cut and tapered, or later in the century given the Neo-classical urn surmounted by a central bowl. Glass baskets hung around the perimeter. Scalloping might appear not only on bowls but also on canopies inspired by the *chinoiserie* of the mid-century.

Glasses for which there seems no obvious use have generally been called water glasses, but in fact there were two distinct kinds which bore this title. One was a tumbler, wide and squat, the other, wider and shallower, was the ancestor of the finger-bowl as seen today. The types in green, amber, amethyst and 'Bristol' blue glass will be well known.*

### WINE-GLASS COOLERS AND MONTEITHS

A glass which looks rather like a finger-bowl, but has either one or two notches in the brim is a wine-glass cooler. I have never seen a picture of this in action, but it is said that you hung a wine glass from the notch, bowl downwards, to await the next wine, so protecting it from the heat of the candle on the table and overhead. They came in matching sets, along with the finger-bowls.

For general use at table there was a large bowl with a scalloped or notched rim which was once taken for a punch-bowl but which now, on the testimony of a Scot writing towards the end of the seventeenth century, seems to have been intended for cooling wine glasses collectively. It was called a Monteith, after a 'fantastical' Scot of that name who wore the bottom of his cloak notched.

### CRUETS AND CONDIMENT SETS

Many eighteenth-century shapes are to be found in miniature in the cruet bottles, which thus stand up in their own right as collectors' items.

Salts appear in the familiar bowl shape raised on three legs, even to the lion's feet so often seen in silver. There is

*See *Bristol Glass* in this series.

also the silver-shape trencher salt, and a group, of rather later date, with a double-ogee bowl. At the end of the century came the familiar boat shape; also a great many with or without stands which might be taken for sweetmeats: perhaps this is what they are.

### FRUIT AND SALAD BOWLS

It is on fruit and salad bowls, one feels, that cutting is most at home. Here the forms are usually simple and do seem to need something more than their own simplicity. Heavy cutting puts light into the glass and gives us the rich effect we look for.

The boat-shaped bowl appeared in the 1770's. There is a very handsome type with a scalloped and crested rim which stands upon a pedestal and is sometimes separable from it. The round affair with a fan escallop border and uncomplicated diamonds is perhaps better called a dish: it would take strawberries without offending our senses.

The round dish gets itself up on to a foot about 1790 and becomes a bowl, for salad perhaps. One also finds in this era a type with a 'kettle-drum rim', or one that is heavily turned down all round. Some of the most elaborate cutting is seen on these bowls, a great many of which were made in the Irish houses. About ten years later it folds down its rim and usually gives another opportunity to show contrasting

*Irish dish with vandyke border and cut all over with lozenge pattern, star cut base.* c. *1790–1800. 14½ in. long.* (Delomosne & Son.)

vertical alternate prisms with diamonds and other motifs. There is, in fact, infinite variety in the scope for cutting on all these bowls. The tall celery vase appears in the early nineteenth century, and again offers fine opportunities for vertical compositions in cutting.

### JUGS AND EWERS

In glass, as in ceramics and silver, jugs and ewers offer some of our best shapes. The Ravenscroft decanter, as we have seen, had more than a hint of the jug; and some interesting dualities were made before the decanter found its final direction.

For me the most attractive of the jugs proper were those made about the middle of the eighteenth century with deep-edge cutting around the rim and lightly cut or incised decoration on the body. Later, about 1780–90, there appeared the Neo-classical, helmet-shaped ewer, with deep scalloping in the rim and shallower notching on the foot-rim. This was a brave affair in its way; and a nice exercise in art history is to compare this late revival of Classicism with Ravenscroft's Renaissance: it is not, one hopes, unkind, to offer the parallel of Wedgwood's Greco-Roman with Classical Greek. But those models which make use of horizontal prisms on the neck add originality and vitality to the form.

Cream jugs are attractive and less expensive than most items. They do not appear to have been made much before about 1740, when the habit, custom and even ritual of tea-drinking had begun to spread down from the aristocracy—who would have been using sets of Dresden or Chantilly porcelain—to the middle classes. There is a shape in the Saffron Walden Museum, on tripod feet, and with a border of threads below the brim, the style of which has been very prettily borrowed from silver: the type is more common without feet. There are also waisted jugs with a pronounced neck and a bulbous body; and another sort with a cylindrical neck and a shouldered body.

*Sweetmeat stand with branches for four candles. c. 1790. 21 in. high.* (Delomosne & Son.)

## ILLUMINATING GLASSWARE

The power of English crystal to disperse and reflect light is shown nowhere more effectively than in the family of 'illuminating glassware'.

It is a large family, and takes one all the way from the humble 'lacemaker's' lamp to the magnificent many-tiered chandelier with its hundreds of flashing cut-glass lustres.

### A. OIL-LAMPS

The little glass oil-lamps are modest things intended to give light to the seamstress, the lacemaker or to the family at their evening meal. The earliest type seems to have consisted of a simple glass bowl on a foot or pedestal: a wick floated in the oil on a disc of cork or copper. Another type has a glass cover with a wick running centrally through it; a third, often taken for a salt, is in double-ogee form, the font or bowl being set upon a flat, wide foot. There is also a lamp in the shape of a wine glass, after which it is called. Later, the font was made separately, with a peg foot which would fit into the socket of any candlestick and so offer an alternative and improved form of lighting to the guttering and smelly tallow candle. These peg lamps, as they are called, were also used in lanterns.

It has been held by some that the peg lamps were also used as light condensers, that the globe was filled not with oil, but with water, and placed beside the candle to reflect and increase the power of its light.

The so-called 'lacemaker's' lamp also appeared in a variety which produced three or four points of light instead of one. From the bowl or font, which was mounted on a foot or pedestal, rose several spouts, each of them with a horizontal lip into which was inserted a metal cap for the wick. They can be, and often are, mistaken for flower holders, and indeed they do look very like some of those seen in Bristol and Dutch delftware.* One begins to wonder, in fact, if some of the latter have not been wrongly classified.

*See *Delftware* in this series.

Although the earlier of these various lamps have such very English features as 'nipt diamond waies' and folded feet, there is something rather French about their form. Perhaps they were made here in glass of lead following the patterns of specimens in potash glass brought over by immigrant Huguenot weavers, lacemakers or lapidaries.

### B. CANDLESTICKS AND TAPERSTICKS

Moving further up the scale we now come to the wide range of glass candlesticks. They show most of the decorative features crystal glass has to offer, and some idea of the sequence of their forms is shown on this page.

In the beginning, as will be seen, candlestick styles tended to follow the styles of silver and pewter rather than other forms of glassware. There was good reason for this: the taller stem called for more variety of knopping and other decoration than, for example, in wine glasses. The earliest forms displayed a high-domed foot, perhaps bell or trumpet-shaped, and the drip tray had an everted rim. About 1700 there appeared a double-domed foot and perhaps fifteen years later the Silesian stem (see below).

The glassmen of the late Stuart times would get length by

*Candlesticks, 1695 onwards:* (Left to right) *Baluster stem, high-domed foot.* c. *1695. 8$\frac{1}{16}$in. Silesian stem, with rings and knop, ribbed and domed foot.* c. *1715–25. 7½ in. Taperstick, with scalloping, cutting in small diamonds and fan-shaped panelling.* c. *1770. 6 in. Column stem, flute moulded, domed foot with terraced rim.* c. *1770. 6 in. Girandole candlestick with diamond and flute cutting in relief, cameo 'sulphide' figure in the stem, hung with pendants.* c. *1820. 11 in.*

*Girandole candlestick.*
(Delomosne & Son.)

having both true and inverted balusters on the same stem. On the taller forms, such as altar candlesticks, they would fill in the space between foot and rim by inverting one stem upon another, repeating the pattern in reverse; the pewterers often did the same. Great use was made of the 'tear' in ball knops; the terraced foot was also strongly featured.

Cut-glass arrived on candlesticks about 1730–40, at first in the form of scalloping on nozzle and footrim. There might be flat diamond facets on the socket and shouldered stems could have vertical fluting. As the century progressed this was extended, and eventually flat cutting and scalloping produced rococo forms to match the current Chippendale. The result was that the candlestick was transformed entirely, as will be seen by the sequence illustrated on page 59.

As in metal, candlesticks in glass showed a gradual widening of the nozzle lip, making it a more effective catcher of dripping wax. By the date of the forms we are now discussing, the lip had expanded into a saucer or sconce, sometimes made separately and fitted into plain nozzles. The early 'tears' were later pulled out into spiral air-twists, earning for these types the trade-name 'worm candlesticks'. There followed opaque enamel-twists, both white and coloured, but neither very prolifically nor very happily. Crystal, when dealing with light, needed no such lily-gildings.

Before passing to the senior members of the lighting family, one must mention a charming junior. It is a version of the candlestick, made with a narrow socket and designed to take the tapers which the Georgian family found so useful for sealing letters, lighting pipes and scenting rooms, which sometimes must have been very necessary in those days. It has been called a tea candlestick, because of its frequent use at the tea table.

For the most part the taperstick followed the candlestick in styles, often being *en suite* as a complete set. It appeals as a smaller version of something else, as do all miniatures, and also because, on the whole, its decoration was rather more restrained than that of the candlestick proper.

### C. VASE CANDLESTICKS AND GIRANDOLES

We move next to the vase candlestick. This seems to have developed in response to the glassmakers' need in the 1770's and 1780's for something heavier to cut. One feature was a lumpy sort of bowl, following the Neo-classical urn. It also had square, solid feet and a deep and cylindrical socket. Here was Adam in glass. Quite apart from carrying out its duties in the way of lighting, the vase candlestick was evidently intended to stand up on its own square feet as an imposing ornament.

This is clearly seen in the next stage, where widening of the drip tray enabled brilliant cut-glass lustres to be hung from it, so reflecting and repeating on their facets the light from the candle above. Later, these could also be hung from the nozzle itself. At first lustres were in the form of pear-drops; then came the well-known 'icicles'. Then the flange was made separately so that it could fit loosely on the stick and revolve; by this stage the girandole, or 'roundabout' candlestick had evolved. In its full maturity it developed into the 'double-cascade' girandole.

*Table candelabra.* (Victoria & Albert Museum.)

D. CANDELABRA AND CHANDELIERS

Another line of development was from candlestick to candelabra. By 1750, in some cases, the stem rose from a broad terraced and cut foot through a deeply diamond-cut baluster up to a tapered spire terminating in a finial which itself had two or three sets of pendant lustres. Arms snaked out to hold the wide drip trays, also hung with shaped lustres, and the full-mouthed sockets stood up like great urns. As in the girandoles, the elaborate cutting of the mid-century appeared alongside the simpler Neo-classical forms, with their elongated, slender columns: these stems are often hexagonal in section, cut with long fluting.

In Regency times the candelabrum took on quite a different over-all look. Generally it consisted of an extremely complicated gathering of pendant icicles and drops arranged in a fringe, but conforming now to a more disciplined outline, usually cylindrical.

Wall lights or sconces—also called girandoles—were made in crystal glass, usually as mirror plates with a socket in which outward-curving branches carried the candles. Sometimes they had several candle arms—perhaps snaked—with spire finials. For these things other kinds of 'illuminaries' were also used: besides the finials and lustres there were canopies, stars, crescents, diamonds and other shapes, first cast in moulds then faceted, usually on one side.

Supreme in the hierarchy of illuminating glassware is the chandelier. There are many magnificent specimens of these still hanging in great rooms, and they reveal to us what several hundred facets of crystal glass can do for light—though nowadays, one suspects, the hard glare of electricity runs a poor second in effectiveness to the soft light of hundreds of wax candles.

Chandeliers appeared first in Venetian *cristallo* in the seventeenth century, and the earliest English ones seem to date from the beginning of the eighteenth. It was here, where expense was of little consequence, that rich cutting and faceting was developed most quickly.

*Chandelier from Wroxton Abbey*. c. *1815*. (Victoria & Albert Museum.)

In early days, perhaps under Italian influence, the chandelier showed good proportions, being evenly balanced in form as between shaft and branching arms, and the smaller decorative features were so controlled as to make a harmonious whole. But as time went on and the glassmen became more and more obsessed with decoration, the emphasis moved to the shaft, which was now given a series of heavily cut balls or globes and a large canopy. Scalloping and hollow cutting were extended to the branches and sockets, and even the pendants had their little spires or spear shafts. Although some of these seem over-ornate to us today, one cannot help admiring their elegance and also the consummate craftsmanship in the making and assembly of the great number and variety of components.

Some of the finest chandeliers in existence—and for that matter some of the best workmanship in lead crystal generally—are those made for the Assembly Rooms at Bath. They were once thought to be of Waterford make, on the grounds, presumably, that everything fine came from that place. But when they were restored under the direction of Mr J. B. Perret, he discovered from a beautifully engraved inscription on the base of a bowl, that they were made by William Parker of Fleet Street, London, a figure who dominated the trade in chandelier making throughout the second half of the eighteenth century.

This technique is carried into even greater elaboration in the great chandelier formerly at Wroxton Abbey, and now in the Victoria and Albert Museum (page 63). Made about 1815, this extraordinary piece of work is six feet in height and four feet wide and is made up of no fewer than 4,500 separate pieces. Its general outline is that of a Neo-classical urn, with festoons of cut drops falling into eight concentric rings in ormolu, hung with pendent icicles. Here, it will be observed, stem and branches have become entirely subservient to decoration and all-over shape.